A Year's Journey:

52 Notes of Growth

Neil J. Parrott

N.J. Parrott Publishing

P.O. Box 10114

Cranston, RI 02910

Book cover: © Neil J. Parrott

Illustrations: © Amejya Parrott, Neil J. Parrott

ISBN: 9798699516025

I'd like to thank my family and friends who inspire me to be the best version of myself. To anyone that feels a little down or unsure of their talents, understand that you are capable of more than anyone can imagine.

Contents

Opening

Several aspects of life can cause us to lose confidence or feel as if all is lost. Even in moments of happiness, we may feel empty or yearn for a sense of belonging. This collection of affirmations is designed to help with bouts of self-doubt, clips of confusion, or spells of indecisiveness. We all could use words of encouragement to help us break through tough times. Even the smallest of gestures can go a long way to boost our confidence. After dealing with some hardships, I came to realize a change of mindset and view of self can work wonders for my self-esteem and emotional being. If I believe in myself and continue moving forward, I can out live the fear of failure or insecurity. It's not the magic bullet that will cure all that is bad, but it docs help turn things around. It does not matter if you are looking for a change in your personal or professional self, this book can be your way of centering yourself time and time again. Let these quotes become more than words on a page; absorb their meanings and embrace their healing power. Use this book as a guide throughout the year and allow it to become part of your journey through each passing week.

As you embark on this journey, just know that there will be many bumps and bruises. But those bumps and bruises are yours to embrace. It's your journey - live it to the fullest.

Section 1: New Beginnings

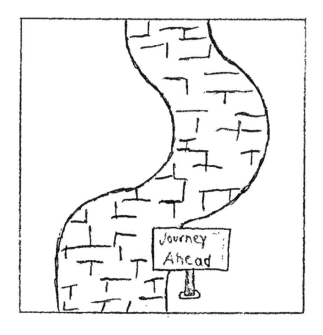

1

Let the mind wander [roam]. It has healing and strengthening effects.

_____

_____

_____

_____

_____

_____

_____

_____

_____

G	
L	
O	
W	

2

Your inner circle should be full of individuals that challenge and make you grow.

G	
L	
O	
W	

<u>3</u>

Don't rely on others to do what only you yourself can. Motivation only goes so far; action by one's self starts the process.

G	
L	
O	
W	

<u>4</u>

It's never too late to start - start today.

_____

_____

_____

_____

_____

_____

_____

_____

_____

_____

G	
L	
O	
W	

The start of a new year brings opportunity of change. Each time our year flips, we make new resolutions or set our eyes on new heights. Just know that newness does not mean erase your past, but rather to become a better version of yourself through uncharted experience which, inevitably, forces us to evolve. It means that a lesson is to be learned or a new badge is to be earned. As said by many, "when one door closes, another one opens." It is with certainty that challenges will arise and require us to become more than our current presence.

Section 2: Preparation

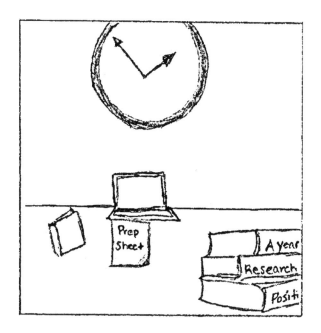

<u>5</u>

If you ever wanted to do something that you thought was out of reach, now is the time to plan out your steps that you can work on to get you there.

_____

_____

_____

_____

_____

_____

_____

_____

_____

G	
L	
O	
W	

<u>6</u>

At any moment you could be called upon. Be ready to rise to the occasion. Set expectations for yourself that are beyond your current state.

_____

_____

_____

_____

_____

_____

_____

_____

_____

G	
L	
O	
W	

7

You have to continuously prepare yourself for what's to come. Thinking once the moment arrives is too late.

_____

_____

_____

_____

_____

_____

_____

_____

G	
L	
O	
W	

<u>8</u>

Opportunity waits for no one. Be ready at all times.

G	

L	

O	

W	

As we seek to identify a way to change our current environment, it is equally important that we understand what it is we aim to adjust. Targeting a specific problem area leads to a greater impact. Once you've identified your target, the next step is to prepare the mind and body for the new ways of being. There will be a need to make decisions that challenge your effort of change. Preparation will help you meet that challenge. While preparation starts the process of creating the next level you, practice begins to build the road of transition.

Section 3: Self-Focus

9

The sun rises and sets each day; a reset cycle. Reset yourself each day to stay grounded and focused.

_____

_____

_____

_____

_____

_____

_____

_____

G	
L	
O	
W	

<u>10</u>

How many times have you bent over backwards to help someone else? Try doing the same for yourself today.

_____

_____

_____

_____

_____

_____

_____

_____

_____

G	
L	
O	
W	

11

They say that you're enough. How about saying to yourself, "I'm more than enough and I'm great with being me.

_____

_____

_____

_____

_____

_____

_____

_____

G	
L	
O	
W	

12

Many times we are worried about satisfying others. Make sure to satisfy yourself first; then you'll be able to function without a feeling of being first.

_____

_____

_____

_____

_____

_____

_____

_____

G	
L	
O	
W	

13

To settle is to accept your current norm and ceiling. Never settle, and always strive for a better self.

_____

_____

_____

_____

_____

_____

_____

_____

_____

G

L

O

W

There are plenty of distractions in our lives that take time away from ourselves. Work, family, and social life all provide distractions in their own way. Work always presents a new deadline; family demands of school visits or doctor's appointments stretch us thin; and friends ask us to join them for random outings. Whether it's big or small, we continuously use time on others that could have been spent on ourselves. We too need to be developed, reenergized, taken care of, and watered. Our mind and body need attention for growth and upkeep, but more importantly, need rest for revival. An overrun body will eventually break down. What good are you to anyone, or yourself for that matter, if you mind and body are not at full performance? Take time for yourself by blocking off sections in your day and stick to it!

Section 4: Mind Adjustment

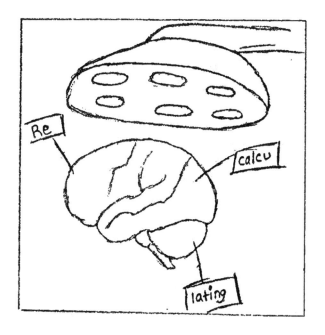

<u>14</u>

The mind is a powerful tool that can help you achieve more than you'd ever imagine. Let it break free from its current limits.

_____

_____

_____

_____

_____

_____

_____

_____

_____

G	

L	

O	

W	

<u>15</u>

Accomplishing goals, overcoming fear, or finding one's self starts with a decision to try.

_____

_____

_____

_____

_____

_____

_____

_____

_____

G	
L	
O	
W	

16

The mind believes what it's told over and over again. So plant seeds of positivity.

G	
L	
O	
W	

<u>17</u>

The only limits you have are the ones you set on yourself. Be limitless.

_____

_____

_____

_____

_____

_____

_____

_____

_____

G	
L	
O	
W	

The mind allows us to experience the world in many ways. We can put ourselves in different 'shoes' and conceptualize various scenarios. The ability to think abstractly is amazing. However, we neglect our inner desire to dream most of the time. We allow societal boundaries to restrict the capabilities of that very gift. Instead of allowing ourselves to float in the clouds of possibility, we limit our thoughts to parameters of the past. Let the mind grow through exercising the muscle and providing proper nourishment. Give yourself space to evaluate your alternate paths. Give yourself some space to ponder your whole self.

Section 5: Patience

<u>18</u>

Timing is everything. Too soon, you miss
the mark. Too late, you miss your chance.
Practice patience and learn the art of the
right time and place.

_____

_____

_____

_____

_____

_____

_____

_____

G

L

O

W

<u>19</u>

Be patient with your expectations. Many do not see the hard work and sacrifice of success. Stick to the plan.

_____

_____

_____

_____

_____

_____

_____

_____

G	
L	
O	
W	

<u>20</u>

Patience is a virtue and hard to consistently practice. Take your time; you'll get there.

_____

_____

_____

_____

_____

_____

_____

_____

_____

G	
L	
O	
W	

21

At times, all it takes is a little down time to find the answer you've been looking for. Be patient.

_____

_____

_____

_____

_____

_____

_____

_____

_____

G	
G	
L	
O	
W	

Not everything comes at the exact time that we want. In fact, almost nothing ever does. Patience truly is a virtue. We must learn to let time run its course for not all aspects of the process can be influenced. Most of the time, patience is referred to as a state of waiting in response to an action of others. Well, it also applies to the action on your part. There will be crossroads in life that will require you to move at the right moment. Thus, patience plays a role in response as well as action. It takes time to master, so practice patience as much as possible. Learn what can be pushed forward and what you have to let run its course. In other words, some things will be out of your hands, so focus your energy on the ones that aren't.

Section 6: Stillness

<u>22</u>

In a fast paced environment, take time to relax and reflect.

_____

_____

_____

_____

_____

_____

_____

_____

G

L

O

W

<u>23</u>

Perfection is an illusion of society. But satisfaction lies within us all. Be satisfied with who you are at all times to obtain your sense of perfection.

_____

_____

_____

_____

_____

_____

_____

_____

G	
L	
O	
W	

<u>24</u>

It never hurts to live in the present. Take a moment to acknowledge what you've accomplished so far. It'll re-energize you for what's to come.

_____

_____

_____

_____

_____

_____

_____

_____

G	
L	
O	
W	

25

Remember to find pockets of quietness in such a busy, noise-filled world.

G	
L	
O	
W	

<u>26</u>

Let your guard down for those who are supportive of your growth for you shall find this to be a major part of becoming more.

_____

_____

_____

_____

_____

_____

_____

_____

_____

G	

L	

O	

W	

Most of life is synched to a fast-paced machine that demands high energy from you. As stated in section 3, numerous "things" fight for your attention. You need to let yourself be a part of today - the right now. Do this by slowing down to a state of stillness. As it is within this stillness that your mind will be allowed to clear. From there, you can then see the whole picture and decide which path you should choose to venture.

Section 7: Failure Happens

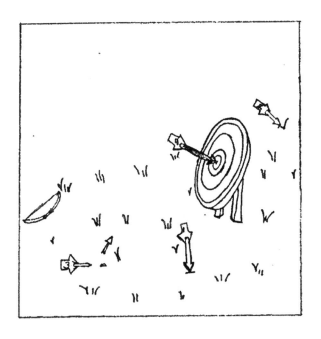

<u>27</u>

Success is not defined by being the first [to finish] or climbing the highest, but how one bounces back from failures.

_____

_____

_____

_____

_____

_____

_____

_____

G	
L	
O	
W	

28

In that moment of doubt remember to embrace the challenge. Growth comes in many forms.

G	
L	
O	
W	

<u>29</u>

Life is about the lessons learned during the
journey. Chances not taken are lessons
undiscovered. Moments not lived are
lessons unknown. Interactions not made
are lessons unspoken

G

L

O

W

<u>30</u>

Failure occurs when a person decides to quit after being faced with a challenge. Many have gone through the struggle of failure and lived to talk about it. You can do the same.

_____

_____

_____

_____

_____

_____

_____

_____

G	
L	
O	
W	

There is no such thing as achieving success without experiencing failure. Failure is bound to occur and, chances are, it will happen more than once. Accepting that fact will help minimize its negative impact on your future endeavors. Failure teaches you many lessons about yourself, such as your level of mental toughness, ability to pivot your approach, or your commitment to finishing what you started. A setback is only a failure if you do not learn from it. You have the opportunity to almost never fail - that choice is yours to make.

Section 8: Perspective

Full

Empty

Amejjap

<u>31</u>

One person says, "This day is taking forever to go by!" Another person says, "This day is going by way too fast!" It's a matter of your attitude and perspective. Strive to be positive and you'll see more benefits each day.

_____

_____

_____

_____

_____

_____

_____

_____

_____

G

L

O

W

32

Change your viewpoint to better understand the topic at hand.

_____

_____

_____

_____

_____

_____

_____

_____

_____

G	
L	
O	
W	

33

It's all in which angle you see the problem from. New perspective can work wonders.

_____

_____

_____

_____

_____

_____

_____

_____

_____

G	
L	
O	
W	

34

Don't let the past views cloud your judgment on future opportunities to grow.

G	
L	
O	
W	

All animate and inanimate objects are actually presented the same to each person. They do not morph or change; it is our individual brains that process them differently. Two people can go through the same experience together, at the same time, but come away with a different perspective. Our realities are filtered through the perspectives gained through past experiences. You may feel that years of forming these perspectives leaves you with a crystallized view. That is not the case. We have the ability to change our perspective through learning and being open-minded. Start with stating you are willing to adapt then make an actual effort to listen and learn.

Section 9: Keep Going

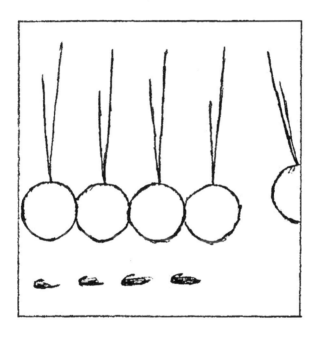

35

There are plenty of reasons to give up, but the reasons to keep going will have the most rewarding long term impact. Keep pushing even if it takes you longer than you had hoped.

_____

_____

_____

_____

_____

_____

_____

_____

G	
L	
O	
W	

36

Make the decision to be better today and
tomorrow will thank you for it.

_____

_____

_____

_____

_____

_____

_____

_____

A YEAR'S JOURNEY

G

L

O

W

89

37

One day you will overcome your doubts, but you must take action now to make it possible.

G

L

O

W

38

There is more to this than sitting back and letting the world decide for you. Go get it.

_____

_____

_____

_____

_____

_____

_____

_____

G

L

O

W

<u>39</u>

Don't stop at the first sign of struggle -
growth does not live there.

_____

_____

_____

_____

_____

_____

_____

_____

_____

G	
L	
O	
W	

The greatest things in life are not free. Reason being there are always sacrifices to be made and long roads to be traveled. No matter how rough the patch or irritating the steps needed to complete the tasks, keep moving forward. Nothing will change if you give up halfway through the journey. You will come to a point in time where you will have to decide whether to continue or stop. In that state of calibration, just remember why you decided to embark upon this journey in the first place. In addition to your why, ask yourself, "what you will gain by continuing and what you will lose by stopping?" If it is something that you still want to accomplish, then you must exhaust all of your options before coming to the end result.

Section 10: Positivity

40

Be the positivity that you wish would be present.

G	
L	
O	
W	

41

A positive mindset works wonders for your outcome in life. Replace thoughts of problems with uplifting ones.

_____
_____
_____
_____
_____
_____
_____
_____
_____

G	
L	
O	
W	

42

Positivity amplifies your efforts and can be
the difference between success and failure.

_____

_____

_____

_____

_____

_____

_____

_____

_____

G

L

O

W

<u>43</u>

Be a positive version of yourself every day.

_____

_____

_____

_____

_____

_____

_____

_____

G	
L	
O	
W	

In life, we are bound to experience anger, sadness, happiness, and gratitude. They are natural responses to some interactions we have in society! These emotions will undoubtedly have an impact on our lives; whether it is positive or negative depends on you. We can all recover from the fallout of our worst emotions, but being negative can really throw you off. Being positive goes a long way. Keep a positive mindset even through the darkest times. You will find that to be uplifting for your spirit and fuel for your actions.

Section 11: Reflection

44

Even the littlest steps add up. Keep doing the small things and then look back at the mountain you created.

G

L

O

W

45

Take a moment to thank a person that helped you recently; someone who was a guiding light during a dark time.

_____

_____

_____

_____

_____

_____

_____

_____

G

L

O

W

46

With each passing day, it gets harder to maintain consistency. Don't worry, soon that nagging task will become one of your most impressive habits.

G	
L	
O	
W	

47

Comparing yourself to peers who don't inspire you to do more will produce lower results. Be different.

_____

_____

_____

_____

_____

_____

_____

_____

_____

G	
L	
O	
W	

As the end of the year approaches, take a look back to see what you've gone through. There have been some ups and some downs but you have been able to keep moving forward. While reflecting on the last 11 months, think about what you may have done differently. Would a change have brought forth a different outcome? Should your time have been invested in a different aspect of your goals? It's okay to not know all the answers; you may never quite be right anyway. [Just taking a second to glance over what you've accomplished can be a breath of fresh air into the last leg of this year.] Reflection helps see the amount of growth as well as areas of opportunity.

Section 12: Forward Thought

48

24 hours in a day: 1/3 spent sleeping. 1/3 spent working. Leaving 8 hours available for miscellaneous tasks. Make the most of it.

_____

_____

_____

_____

_____

_____

_____

_____

G	
L	
O	
W	

49

Every day brings a new opportunity, so prepare today for tomorrow's Journey.

G

L

O

W

50

Keep a "be great" mindset for everything you do.

G

L

O

W

51

Being present or looking back can only happen after setting a vision for which to aspire.

G

L

O

W

<u>52</u>

The last leg of accomplishing your goal is always the hardest. Remember why you started in the first place to get you through.

_____

_____

_____

_____

_____

_____

_____

_____

G	
L	
O	
W	

NEIL J. PARROTT

You have completed another chapter in your life's story. You have made it through some tough times and enjoyed moments of happiness. Now the time has come to think ahead. Set the stage for next year and beyond. You should now have a better idea of your strengths as well as your weaknesses. Let this help you gain an understanding of future expectations.

Closing

Another year is in the books; 52 weeks all leading up to the starter's blocks of the next one. I hope that you were able to become more confident in yourself and that these passages helped you in times of need. Although this book is formatted to flow through the weeks of the year, I hope that you keep it close by for future reference. This way, you can open it up to your favorite quote; or to find words that you really need to hear about how to love and accept yourself. It is not easy traveling along the road of failure, or even sustained success for that matter. No one is immune to feelings of sadness or self-doubt, so I hope you found solace in those vulnerable moments. If there is one lesson to take from this year's journey, let it be your ability to embrace all that is you. For that will feed positivity into other parts of your life by ways of which you have not been open to before.

Tomorrow hasn't happened yet, but today sets its course.

Thank you for reading. Feel free to post a book review. Follow and connect on Instagram @parrottspeaks to share your thoughts and experience.

Made in the USA
Middletown, DE
13 July 2023

35087293R00083